ON EASTERN CROSSROADS

ON EASTERN CROSSROADS

CROSSROADS

LEGENDS AND PROPHECIES OF ASIA

AGNI YOGA SOCIETY

2017

Agni Yoga Society
319 West 107th Street
New York NY 10025
www.agniyoga.org

First published in 1930 by Frederick A. Stokes Company under
the pseudonym Josephine Saint-Hilaire.
Second edition 1992, published by Agni Yoga Society under the
name Helena Roerich.
Third edition 2017, published without the author's name, as
originally intended by Helena Roerich.

FOREWORD TO THE FIRST EDITION

IN the traditions of all peoples there have been legends of pilgrims who set stones along their path in order to find their way back to the source. "On Eastern Crossroads," by Josephine Saint-Hilaire, may be regarded in this light, and we feel that each of these superb fragments so carefully gathered by her adds its sparks to the texture of truth, and reveals the steps of the most ancient traditions. In the variety of subjects, in the work, there is no feeling of a personal impress; it is like a wreath of flowers, gathered not with special concern for the specimens, but out of love for the beauty of the entire meadow. One may feel how during many travels each new contribution to the work was added without any negative thought, and thus was gradually filled the collector's bag of benevolence.

It is valuable to feel that no one is urged to accept these traditions in any one direction. But readers may be enriched in their intuition regarding the constructive aspects of the story of mankind. Thus we see how the minds of the nations collected and preserved for ages the great images as evolving sparks of their genius.

These sparks should be guarded with equal solicitude by ourselves and our posterity. It is chiefly necessary that we should regard with reverence these traditions, nor demean them, but let us apply them to our spiritual necessities in the most constructive and most appreciative way. Thus, let the travelers from the past salute the future!

Often the so-called Apocrypha preserve many traces of reality taken from authentic texts. In these unexpected tales and parables scattered among the peoples of Asia we learn precisely what images live in the folk consciousness.

From Altai to Ceylon people dream of the Great Teachers, recalling from antiquity fragments of their lives and bringing the tale closer to the character of their country.

To gather these Cryptograms of the great thought means to glimpse the souls of the peoples.

CONTENTS

A PAGE FROM THE SACRED HISTORY OF THE LORD BUDDHA

FROM THE LIFE OF CHRIST

THE MOTHER OF THE WORLD

APOLLONIUS OF TYANA

FROM THE LIFE OF ST. SERGIUS OF RADONEGA

AKBAR THE GREAT

LEGENDS AND LORE

PRINCE OF DARKNESS

GOLD AND DARKNESS

LEGEND OF THE STONE

PROPHECIES OF SHAMBHALA AND MAITREYA

A PAGE FROM
THE SACRED HISTORY OF
THE LORD BUDDHA

THE BEGINNING OF THE PATH

THE Lord Buddha verily left the town of His birth. Verily He meditated beneath the tree of wisdom. Verily He taught in Benares. Verily He concluded his teaching in Kushinagar. But the centuries have added their many tales.

The Lord departed from His native place on horseback accompanied by a servant-courier. The road lay north-west, along the valley of the river. The hurried journey lasted for two weeks. Beyond the mountain passes, the trail for horses ended. Further on, the hunter's path continued.

Here the courier left him, but in farewell said, "Prince, Brother, when you will reach the hunter's hut, give him this chip of wood." And he gave him a piece of wood with three signs.

For seven days the Lord traveled the path. Upon the eighth day he reached a hut. The door stood open and a tall old man dressed in a dirty old surplice chipped some wood.

The Lord approached him in greeting, as is the custom of India. But the hunter laughed and pointed to the tree. The Lord remembered the piece of wood and handed it to him. The old man carefully examined the signs and then pointed kindly to the table inside the hut. The Lord understood the invitation and partook of the venison and honey. Then the old man, by gestures, bade the Lord rest.

When Lord Buddha awoke, the sun had just illumined the snow. The hunter was not in the hut, but from the courtyard the strokes of his ax resounded. Soon, however, his figure appeared at the door and he offered to the Lord a drink of honey. Then the old man took a sack and a spear and pointed to the sun. The Lord understood it was time to depart and taking His staff left the hut. The old man bowed thrice before Him and indicated that He should follow.

Approaching the brush he pushed aside the branches and disclosed a narrow path. He beckoned to the Lord to follow him and quickly strode forward, pointing to the sun. Thus they walked until midday. The forest became less dense and the rumble of the river could be heard. They emerged at the river's shore.

The old man arched his bow and shot an arrow. They awaited in silence. The Lord took off His remaining adornments and offered them to the old man. But the latter indicated to cast them in the river.

On the opposite shore a tall man appeared, pushed out his bark and set out in their direction. His garment was edged with fur. And his face was quite dark and broad. Reaching the shore the stranger bowed to the Lord and invited Him into the bark.

The Lord wished to bid farewell to the hunter but he had disappeared unnoticed. The stranger also preserved his silence. Reaching the shore they mounted horses and began to ascend the mountain.

During the night they reached the boundary of snows and at dawn descended into the Abode.

THE PREDESTINED MAITREYA

THE eyes of the child Prince opened early to the miracles of the world. Naught escaped his penetrative attention.

The King said, "Perception is the crown of the Lord, but the strength of His arm is His shield. Let Him strengthen His arm with the bow. Let the children of the noble Kshatriyas compete with the Prince."

The Queen Mother added, "If penetration is the crown of the Lord, and the strength of His arm is His shield, then the glory of the Lord is His mercy and His wisdom. I would that my near one should be surrounded by the Devas of Wisdom who created the Vedas."

Then an old sage turned to the King saying, "Reverend Mother, and thou, Lord, command me to combine your wishes. Command me to bring unto you her whom we call the daughter of the Great Nag, whom we have sheltered in our house. And for seven years have we marveled at her wisdom and the strength of her bow. Verily she is worthy of the hand which has inscribed the wisdom of the Vedas."

"Let her be brought here," commanded the King.

The wise councilor brought a young being, saying, "Maitri, send the worthiest greeting to our King."

Unheard of was it to see a seven-year-old girl in a white garment, her bow and arrow in hand and a dagger in her girdle. The crown of heavy dark hair was not restrained by the fillet of the Nag and the eyes peered out sadly and sternly.

The King said, "Maitri, if you can send the arrow, transfix yonder peacock."

Maitri bowed to the King and said, "I may not take life from an animal; but permit me, King, to pierce an apple on the top of the apple tree."

The King commanded Maitri to be companion to the Prince and greatly admired the wisdom of her who was found on the shores of the lake.

Many years did the Prince spend with Maitri, calling her at times Stern One, or Glowing One, or Warrior, or Seeress of the Wisdom of Nagi.

Maitri opened before him the door of the Path.

When the powerful Lion returned and with the roar of Truth mantled the mountains, Maitri guarded for Him his best pupil and pronounced, "She shall glorify the sight of Thy labors."

The Lord of Truth answered, "Maitri, manifested Councilor and Keeper. Thou who hast hidden thy wisdom from the crowd. Thou shalst assume My place as the Lord of Compassion and Labor. Maitreya shall lead the nations towards Light. And the arrow of achievement shall bestow the apple of Knowledge."

What has been said is as true as that the Temple of Knowledge shall be erected near the site of the glorification of the Teacher.

What has been said is as true as that the pupil of

the Blessed One shall give her name to the Temple of Knowledge.

The base of the manifestation of Truth is affirmed by the labors of life.

Given in Chorten-Karpo.

DEPARTURE

WHEN the time came for departing, the Blessed One said to His Wife, "Let us go."

And thrice he said, "Through the darkness of night, in the midday heat and in the ray of dawn."

But at night the tigers roared and in the heat the snakes crawled forth and towards morning the monkeys came in hordes.

"I am still afraid now," said the wife.

"This is also for the good," said the Blessed One. "Without a call, by your own steps will you be bearer of the Teaching."

And the elephant trumpeted seven times, proclaiming the date of the next meeting.

COMMANDS

"WELL I praise thee, Ananda. Because without call walks She who affirms."

And the Blessed One perceived in the Heaven upon a veil the destiny of the Light of the Mother of the World.

Here the Blessed One says, "All for everything forever."

"Observe four laws: The Law of Containment, the Law of Fearlessness, the Law of Approach and the Law of Benevolence."

THE ELECTED FOR ACHIEVEMENT

HOW did Buddha elect disciples for achievement? During work, when fatigue already possessed the disciples, Buddha asked the most unexpected question, awaiting the promptest reply.

Or placing the simplest object before them, He suggested that they describe it in not more than three words or not less than one hundred pages.

Or setting a pupil before a sealed door, He asked, "How will you open it?"

Or ordering musicians beneath the window, He made them simultaneously sing hymns of entirely dissimilar contents.

Or noticing an annoying fly, He asked the pupil to repeat words unexpectedly pronounced.

Or passing in front of the pupils, He would ask them how many times He had done so.

Or noticing fear of animals or of natural phenomena, He set them the condition to master it.

Thus the powerful Lion tempered the blade of the spirit.

BUDDHA'S FAVORITE PASTIME WITH HIS DISCIPLES

AND one should not forget the favorite pastime of Buddha with His disciples during moments of rest.

The Teacher cast into space one word, on the base of which the disciples built an entire thought.

There is no wiser test of the condition of consciousness.

THE FOUNDATION OF THE TEACHING

PEOPLE do not comprehend the foundation of the Teaching of the Blessed One—the foundation is discipline. Spiritually and physically the monk of the community strove to remain on the path. The first years he endured a severe probation. He was forbidden to kill himself with ascetic practices. But he was ordained to lead the battle by the one origin of the spirit.

Thus austerely did Buddha instruct His disciples.

Verily they knew joy only in the spiritual battle. Hence are the thorns of the path spoken of.

Only when the will of the disciple was engendered as a lion and the silvery rein of spirit held its glow over the feelings of the pupil, then only did the Lord cautiously open the curtain and assign a task.

And gradually the pupil was initiated into the Mysteries of Knowledge.

THE RENUNCIATION OF POSSESSION

O NCE a pupil asked the Blessed One:
"How shall one understand the fulfilment of the Covenant regarding the renunciation of property? One disciple renounced all things but the Teacher continued to reproach him for possession. Another one remained surrounded with objects but did not merit reproach."

"The feeling of possession is measured not by objects but by thought. One may have objects and still not be a possessor."

Buddha always advised to have as few objects as possible in order not to expend too much time upon them.

THE CONDEMNATION OF FANATICS

BUDDHA addressed the Brahmins: "To what has your isolation brought you? In order to procure bread you go to the general market and you value the coins from the bag of a Sudra. Your isolation may be termed simply plunder. And your sacred objects are simply instruments of deception.

"Are not the possessions of the rich Brahmins a desecration of the Divine Law? You consider the south as light and the north as darkness. A time shall come when I will come from the midnight and your light shall be extinguished. Even the birds fly north to bear their young. Even the gray geese know the merit of earthly possession. But the Brahmin tries to fill his girdle with gold and to hoard his treasures under his hearth and under his threshold.

"Brahmin, you lead a contemptible life and your end shall be pitiable. You shall be the first to be visited with destruction.

"If I go northward, then shall I also return from there."

THREE ARHATS

THREE Arhats persistently besought Buddha to permit them to test the power of miracle. Buddha assigned each of them to a dark room and locked them in. After a considerable time the Blessed One called them out and asked them what they had seen. Each related his different visions.

But Buddha said, "Now one must agree that miracles are useless because the supreme miracle you have not perceived. Because you could have sensed existence beyond the visible. And this sensation could have brought you beyond the limits of earth.

"But you continued to realize yourselves as seated on earth and your thought attracted waves of the elements to earth. The inflation of the elemental images evoked cataclysms in various lands. You shattered rocks and destroyed ships in the gale.

"You, for instance, have seen a red beast with a flaming crest. But the fire evoked by you from the abyss demolished the houses of the defenseless ones. Go and help!

"You saw the lizard with the face of a maiden. You impelled the waves to wash away the boats of the fishermen. Hurry to bring help!

"And you have seen the eagles in flight and the whirlwind has destroyed the harvest of the toilers. Go and repay them!

"Then where, Arhats, is your usefulness? The owl in the hollow of the tree has spent its time to greater use. Either you labor on earth with the perspiration of your brow or at the moment of seclusion exalt yourself above the earth. But let not senseless invocation of the elements be the occupation of a sage!"

Verily, the feather which falls from the wing of a tiny bird creates thunder in the far-off worlds.

SHEPHERD AND SANNYASIN

A SHEPHERD beheld a man seated in meditation beneath a tree. Seating himself beside the man, he tried in emulation also to think.

He began to count his goats and mentally to figure out the profit from the sale of the wool.

Both sat silent. Finally the shepherd said, "Lord, of what are you thinking?" "Of God," answered the man.

The shepherd asked, "Do you know of what I was thinking?"

"Also of God."

"You are mistaken. I thought of the profit from the sale of my wool."

"Verily, also of God. But my God has nothing to barter. Yours must first go to the market. Perhaps on the way He may meet a robber who will help him to turn to this tree."

Thus spoke Gautama.

Go to the bazaar. Think quicker in order to return.

THE TRADER OF MONKEYS

ON a ship traveled a trader of monkeys. In his leisure he taught them to imitate the sailors in spreading their sails.

But a storm arose and the sailors hastened to lower their sails. The monkeys, knowing only how to spread the sails, followed the sailors and hoisted them again.

The ship was lost because the trainer foresaw only clear weather.

Thus related Buddha, the Restorer of the Lotus of Life.

A PARABLE ABOUT THE ONE WHO QUESTIONED

GULNOR was considered the wisest one. He had the happiness to find a Teacher who came from the Sacred Subterranean Land, but who was bereft of his tongue and right hand.

The pupil, constantly aspiring, asked a question and the Teacher nodded.

The pupil asked two questions and the Teacher nodded twice.

Soon the pupil asked incessant questions and the Teacher unceasingly nodded. Three years the questions continued and for three years the Teacher nodded.

"Then according to thy experience everything can happen?"

And the Teacher not only nodded but bowed to the ground and opening his garment at the breast, revealed on his bosom the image of the Blessed One bestowing with both hands.

Thus was affirmed wisdom. And the creation of life was exalted.

THE WHEEL OF THE LAW

THE Blessed One told the Parable about the Wheel of the Law. To a skilful copyist came a revered man who gave him the task of copying an appeal to the Lord for which he brought sufficient parchment.

Immediately after, a man came with the request to copy a letter full of threats and also gave a parchment urging that the work be finished quickly.

In order to give the latter preference the copyist changed the rotation and hurried with the second order, taking the parchment of the first one in his haste.

He of the threats was highly pleased and hastened to pour out his venom.

Then came the first customer and looking at the parchment said, "Where is the parchment which I gave?" On hearing what had occurred he said, "The parchment for the prayers bore the blessing of fulfilment whereas the parchment of threats was devoid of effect.

"Unfaithful man. In violating the law of dates you have bereft prayer of its power which could have aided the sick. But above this, you have brought into action threats which are full of unparalleled consequences.

"The labor of the Arhat in blessing my parchment is wasted. Wasted is the labor of the Arhat who stripped evil of its power. You liberated a malicious curse into the world. It will inevitably react upon yourself. You have pushed from the way the Wheel of Law and it will not lead you but will break your way."

Do not write laws upon a dead parchment which will be carried away by the first thief who approaches.

Carry the Laws in spirit and the breath of Benevolence will carry before you the Wheel of the Law illumining your path.

The unreliability of the copyist may bring catastrophe upon the whole world.

THE SENSE OF NECESSITY

WHENCE originated the controversy between Buddha and Devadatta?

Devadatta asked, "Wherefrom to begin each action?"

The Blessed One answered, "From the most necessary. Because each moment contains its necessity and this is called the justice of action."

Devadatta persisted, "How is the evidence of necessity ascertained?"

The Blessed One answered, "The thread of necessity crosses all worlds but whoever has failed to realize it will remain within a dangerous chasm unsheltered from the stones."

Thus Devadatta could not distinguish the line of necessity and this darkness impeded his way.

THE SEEKER FOR BUDDHA

ONE pure man wished to see Buddha. By keeping his attention upon a wide variety of objects his hands did not embrace wise images and his eyes did not penetrate objects of reverence —the manifestation did not come.

Finally, the seeker, bending low in prayer, felt how the thread of a web descended on his forehead. He cast it away. Then a clear voice rang out, "Why dost thou reject My hand? My Ray hast followed thee. Permit Me to embrace thee."

Then the sun-serpent became atremble in the man, and he sought the rejected thread. And in his hands it turned into forty pearls. And each bore the Image of Buddha. In their center was a stone and upon it the inscription, "Valor— despair—joy."

The follower of Buddha received joy because he knew the path to it.

TO THE GREAT ILLUMINED

TO Him of the great Illumination came a pupil, seeking a miracle, "After the miracle, I shall have faith."

The Teacher smiled sadly and revealed to him a great miracle.

"Now," exclaimed the pupil, "I am ready to pass through the steps of the Teaching under thy guidance."

But the Teacher, pointing to the door, said: "Go! I no longer need you."

THE RESCUE OF MAN

THE Blessed One sat above the waters of a deep lake. In the depths one could discern an entire world of fish and seaweed.

The Blessed One noticed how this world resembled kingly palaces. "If man would sink there, with the soles of his feet he would destroy these ephemeral palaces but he himself would choke. Out of such depths the spirit of man does not rise.

"But," smiled the Teacher, "for everything there is a remedy. One can break through the rock and drain the lake. The snails will have either to dry up or find another place of existence. But man will not perish."

The cradle of an infant is like the shell of a snail. Give the children air. Do not permit them to crave objects of their kin, but let each child meet the sun without a trail of tatters.

PARABLE OF THE KING OF MARAGOR

THUS spoke the Blessed One to Narada.

The Lord of Jataka said to his favorite Councilor, "Know you the work of the King of Maragor? Have you heard his name? Are his deeds familiar to you?"

The Councilor, peering about, whispered, "Lord, this evil name is unutterable! All Darkness conceals the traces of his deeds."

"I give you a mission. Gather a hundred trusty men and find means resourcefully to traverse the Lands of Maragor. Describe to me minutely all his customs. And if you encounter the King himself, tell him I do not fear to pronounce his name."

Ten years passed. The Councilor returned, wiser in countenance but filled with confusion. By now not one hundred but a thousand accompanied him.

"Lord, much labor did I spend, to which a thousand witnesses are before you. But the task is unfulfilled. Endlessly we questioned the people; numberless were the countries we traversed. I say to you, Lord, the most startling—the King of Maragor does not exist nor do his evil customs!"

"Good," said the Lord. "Can you take an oath by your words?" — "Before you are a thousand and one oaths."

"Then take your witnesses and walk through all squares and temples. Proclaim and inscribe on the pillars that which you pronounce.

"My son, you fulfilled the mission. By your labors you smote the beast of darkness. The phantom of fright vanished, for no one fears that which is known.

"Maragor is revealed as the fear of mankind and is annihilated by the labors of valor and devotion. Be my son; you have destroyed the darkness!"

PRECEPTS TO THE RULER
OF RAJAGRIHA

ONCE the Blessed One visited the Ruler of Rajagriha. The Ruler called attention to the immaculateness of his reception room. But the Blessed One said, "Better show the cleanliness of your sleeping chamber, of your bath and your hearth. The reception room is contaminated by many unworthy ones. But there where your consciousness is created, let it be spotless."

And the Blessed One said, "Distinguish between those who understand and those who agree. He who understands the Teaching shall not tarry in applying it to life. He who agrees will nod and extol the teaching as remarkable wisdom but will not apply this wisdom to life.

"Many have agreed but like a withered forest they are fruitless and without shade. Only decay awaits them. Those who understood are few but like a sponge they drink in the precious knowledge and are ready to cleanse the horrors of the world with the sacred liquid.

"He who understands cannot but apply the Teaching, because realizing goal-fitness he accepts it as a solution of life.

"Do not waste time with the agreeing ones; let them first demonstrate the application of the first call."

Thus is attributed to the Blessed One the goal-fitting attitude to the newcomers.

FROM THE LIFE OF CHRIST

THE STAR

WHAT Star was it that guided the Magi? Of course it was the Command of the Brotherhood: To hail Jesus, to safeguard, and to bring some means to the poor family.

We walked over the face of the earth not knowing the exact spot. The Commands of the Teraphim directed us or led us from day to day. When we heard, "It is near!", we had just lost all signs of habitation.

Could one expect a miracle of so unprecedented an Annunciation in the midst of camel dung and the braying of donkeys? Human thought attempted to locate the future prophet perhaps near a temple or at least majestic walls.

We received the Command to halt at a humble inn. In the low-ceilinged house with clay walls we stopped for the night. A fire and a small oil lamp filled the room with a red glow.

After our meal we noticed that a servant poured out the remains of the milk into a separate amphora. We said to her, "It is not right to save it." "But," she said, "it is not for Thee, O Lord, but for a poor woman. Here behind the wall lives a carpenter. Recently a son was born to him."

Extinguishing the fire, we laid on our hands and asked, "Whither shall we go further?" Came the answer, "Nearer than the nearest. Lower than the lowest. Higher than the highest." Not understanding the meaning we besought a Command, but we were told, "Let the ears hearken."

And we sat in the darkness in silence. And we heard how somewhere beyond the wall a child had begun to cry. We began to mark the direction of the cry and we heard the Mother's song so often heard in the homes of husbandmen: "Let people count thee a plower, but I know, my son, thou art a king. Who, save thee, shall raise the best seed, the most fruitful. The Lord shall call my little one and say, 'Thy seed alone hast glorified My feast. Sit with Me, king of the worthiest seeds.' "

As we heard this song three knocks resounded in the ceiling. We said, "In the morning we shall go there."

Before dawn we donned our finest garments and besought the servant to lead us in the direction of the cry. She said, "The Lord wishes to visit the family of the carpenter. I had better lead you around for here one must pass through the cattle fold." Recalling the Command, we chose the shortest way.

Here behind the manger was a tiny dwelling leaning against rock. Here by the hearth was a woman and in her arms—He. What signs accompanied? He stretched out His little hand and on the palm was a red sign. Upon this sign we placed the most precious pearl of those we brought.

Bestowing the treasures and the sacred objects, we warned the mother of the need of wanderings and at once we turned back crossing the same manger.

Behind us the mother said, "See, my little one, thou

art the king. Set this diamond upon the forehead of thy steed."

We departed bearing in mind the sign of the red star upon the palm.

Then, also, had been said, "Remember the day of the red star upon the forehead of the warrior."

THE WAY OF CHRIST

THUS shall we begin the story of His life, that the unmutilated word shall be inscribed upon earth.

For thirty years He walked repeating the word so as to impart it to those who would not receive it. The Teachings of Buddha, of Zoroaster, and the old sayings of the Vedas, He learned upon the crossroads.

Perceiving pure eyes, He asked, "Know you aught of God?"

By river barges He awaited the travelers and asked, "Do you bear aught for me?" For it was need that He cross with human feet and ask with human words.

When He was told of the starry signs He asked to know their verdicts; but the alphabet had no attraction for Him; people did not exist for this. "How can I calm the devastating storm? How can I disclose the heaven to men?

"Why are they rent from the eternal existence to which they belong?"

Such teaching of the essence of life effaced methods of magic because instead of winning the subservience of the minor spirits of nature He razed all obstacles with the sword of His spirit. His teaching guided the people to the possibilities of the spirit. Therefore there were no prophets near Him but only by the stars one knew of Him.

We knew much and He was all-able. Then we resolved to serve His Teaching.

THE ARRIVAL OF CHRIST

ONE should remember the day of the most joyless offering—Christ who only gave, accepting nothing. This determination from an early age brought Him across a scorching desert. And His Feet burned as those of a simple driver.

We awaited Him. But as usual, the moment of His coming was unexpected. A horse had been brought to Me and I was bidding farewell to My family when a servant noticed a ragged traveler. His slender face was pale, and His hair hung in wavy locks below His shoulders. And only a gray sack-cloth covered His body. I did not even see a gourd for drinking.

But My wife went first to meet Him, and when afterwards I asked her why she had hastened, she said, "It seemed as though a star glowed in my bosom, and the heat, even to pain, burst into rays." For the Traveler was already exalted as He approached the tent. Then I understood Who had come.

After crossing the desert He partook only of corn bread and a cup of water and soon asked, "When shall We depart?"

I replied, "When the Star permits." And We awaited the sign of the Star. He was silent repeating only, "When?" And marking the Star, I said, "There is blood in Pisces." He only nodded.

Thus for three years daily We awaited. And the light of the Star shone over Us.

I recall He spoke somewhat of a vision of Light in which a small boy brought Him a sword. And when Light, as a Rainbow, was poured before Him, a soundless Voice bade Him go.

I was told to accompany Him, where I Myself was not yet to enter.

On a white camel We set out by night. And by night-crossing We reached Lahore where We found a follower of Buddha, apparently expecting Us.

Never have I seen such resolution because We were on Our way for three years.

We awaited Him and brought Him to Jordan. Again a white sack-cloth covered Him. And again He set forth alone under the morning Sun. And a Rainbow shone over Him.

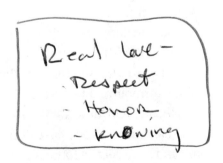

THE SIGNS OF CHRIST

THE Star of Allahabad pointed out the way. And so We visited Sarnath and Gaya. Everywhere We found the desecration of religion. On the way back under the full moon occurred the memorable saying of Christ.

During the night-march the guide lost his way. After seeking I found Christ seated upon a sand-mound looking at the sand flooded by moon-light.

I said to Him, "We have lost Our way. We must await the indication of the stars."

"Rossul M., what is a way to Us when the whole world is awaiting Us?"

Then taking His bamboo staff He traced a square round the impression of His foot, saying, "Verily, I say, by human feet."

Then making the impression of His palm He also surrounded it with a square, "Verily by human hands."

Between the squares He drew the semblance of a pillar surmounted by an arc.

He said, "Oh, how Aum shall penetrate into the human consciousness! Here I have drawn a pistil and above it an arc and have set the foundation in four directions. When, by human hands and human feet, the Temple shall be built wherein will blossom the pistil laid by Me, then let the builders pass by My way. Why shall We await the way when it is before Us?"

Then rising, He effaced with His cane all which He had drawn.

"When the Name of the Temple shall be pronounced then shall the inscription emerge. In remembrance of My constellation, the square and nine stars shall glow over the Temple. The sign of the foot and the hand will be inscribed above the Keystone." Thus He Himself spoke on the eve of the New Moon.

And the heat of the desert was great.

THE STORY OF MARY MAGDALENE

YOU know my way of life, how by night they knew us and by day averted their glances. So with Christ. By night they came and by day they averted their glances. I thought, "Here am I, the lowest, and by sunlight they are ashamed of me. But He, the most exalted prophet, is also avoided by day. Thus are the lowest and the highest equally avoided."

And so I decided to find him by day and to stretch out my hand to Him. I donned my best attire and my necklace from Smyrna and perfumed my hair. And so I went, to say to people, "Here by day are met the lowest and the highest, equally avoided by you."

And when I saw Him seated among the fishermen and covered with a sack-cloth, I remained on the opposite side and could not approach. Between us, people passed, equally avoiding us.

Thus my life was determined. Because He said to His most beloved disciple, "Take this pinch of dust and bring it to this woman that she may exchange it for her necklace. Verily in these ashes is more life than in her stones, because from ashes I can create stones but from stones only dust."

The rest you already know. Because He did not condemn me. He but weighed my chains and the chains of shame crumbled like dust.

He decided simply. Never did He hesitate to send the simplest object which determined one's entire life. He touched these sendings as though bathing them in spirit.

His path was empty because people, after receiving His gifts, hastily departed. And wishing to lay on His hands, He found all empty.

When He was already condemned, the furies of shame rushed behind Him and mockingly brandished their branches. The price of the robber was worthy of the crowd.

Verily He cleft asunder the chains because He bestowed knowledge without accepting reward.

THE SCRIBES

NIGHT fell. Christ sat upon the threshold.
A scribe passed and asked, "Why dost thou sit at the by-way?"

Christ answered, "Because I am the threshold of the Spirit. If thou wouldst pass, pass through Me."

Another scribe asked, "Is it true that the Son of David sits at the place for dogs?"

Christ answered, "Verily thou defamest David, My Father."

It became dark and the third scribe asked, "Why sitteth thou as if fearful of thy house?"

Christ answered, "I await that the night-darkness should free Me from sight of thee. Verily, darkness, depart unto darkness."

Then rising, He pointed to Mount Moriah whereon stood the Temple, and said, "My Grandfather created the Temple of stone but He sits under the linen of the tent."

Said the scribe, "Mad man, He believes that Solomon still lives."

And they departed in ignorance.

Afterwards Mary came out of the house and seeing Christ said, "Master, share our evening meal."

Christ answered, "The gift of the heart glows through the darkness."

THE QUESTIONER OF CINEDRION

A MEMBER of Cinedrion asked Christ, "Would you come to us if we should ask you?"

Christ answered, "Better would I go to the cemetery for there is no lie."

A member of Cinedrion asked Christ, "Why dost thou not acknowledge us if even Thy father was married by one of our members?"

"Wait until your house crumbles; then shall We come."

"Wherefore shalt thou come—to destroy or to erect?"

"Neither for destruction nor erection but for purification. Because I shall not return to the old hearth."

"How then, not to respect your forefathers!"

"New cups are given for the feast. Respecting a grandfather, one need not drink out of his cup."

EYES—OPEN WOUNDS

TO CHRIST was shown an image from a distant land. On the palms and on the feet were open eyes.

One asked, "Is it not superstition? Can one see through the hands and the soles of the feet?"

The Teacher said, "Verily we learn to see by the hand and the foot. Will the sluggard know the essence of things? How shall we express our conclusions if we shall not apply our hands? And by our feet the spirit treads through earth."

Then the Teacher added, "Wise ones gave this image in order to recall the nature of things."

And He also added, "Are not these eyes like open wounds? Verily, verily, through open Wounds comes the light."

THE MOTHER OF THE WORLD

- Mental Health
is union w/ self
- & then take action
based on that union

Don't grow beyond
arrive — we deteriorate it

THE MOTHER OF THE WORLD

THE Mother of the World hides Her Face. The Mother of the World veils Her Face.

The Mother of the Lords is not a symbol but a Great Manifestation of the Feminine Origin in which is revealed the spiritual Mother of Christ and Buddha—She Who taught and ordained Them to achievement.

From times immemorial the Mother ordained achievement. Through the history of humanity Her Hand traces the unbreakable thread.

Her voice rang out on Sinai. She assumed the image of Kali. Seek Her behind Isis and Ishtar.

After Atlantis, when Lucifer flung his blow at the cult of spirit, the Mother of the World began a new thread.

After Atlantis the Mother of the World veiled Her Image and forbade the pronunciation of Her Name until the Hour of the Constellations would strike.

THE EFFULGENCE OF
THE MOTHER OF THE WORLD

THE purple aura of the Mother of the World bathes us. Who shall not bow? Who shall dare against Her?

Among the predestined treasures are guarded her lustrous adornments. The Teaching of Her glows as a purple Lotus.

Let the pain of the center of the solar plexus be linked with Her Days.

Let the new coils of the Serpent unfurl during Her Days. Let the trumpets of air herald Her Time.

Mother of the World, pass over the desert, because the flowers are behind Thee! Mother of the World, look upon the Mountains, because they glow with Thy Fire!

Departed are the despicable ones. The hordes are rising.

New miracles. New bearers. And above the destruction of the walls rises the voice, "Mother approaches!"

"Mother of Buddha! Mother of Christ! Inspire Thy Sons!

"Even though a rock fall upon me, yet shall I know that it comes from Thy Steps."

Thus shall we flood space.

THE COMMAND

AND above all spoken commands rings out the Silent Command—All-penetrating, Immutable, Indivisible, Irrevocable, Effulgent, All-Bestowing, Unutterable, Irrepeatable, Invulnerable, Inexpressible, Timeless, Undeferable, Illuminating, Manifest in Lightning.

Here are two Commands—at the limits of the World are the Lords Christ and Buddha. And Their Word is as a Flaming Sword. But above them is manifest a Silent Command.

Above Them is She Who veiled Her Face, She Who wove the Web of the far-off worlds, She the Envoy of the Unutterable, the Ruler of the Intangible, the Bestower of the Unrepeatable.

By Thy Command is the Ocean Silenced and the whirlwinds trace the invisible signs.

And She Who Veiled Her Face shall stand Alone in Vigil, amid the Splendor of Her Signs.

And none shall mount the Summit. None shall witness the Effulgence of the Dodecahedron, the Sign of Her Power.

Out of the spiral of Light, She herself has woven the Sign in Silence. She, the Guide of those who go towards attainment!

The four squares of the sign of affirmation are bestowed by Her upon those who determined to achieve.

THE PLAY OF THE MOTHER OF THE WORLD

HOW great is the play of the Mother of the World! She beckons to her children from far-distant fields.

"Hasten, children! I wish to teach you. I have keen eyes and alert ears ready for you. Sit ye down upon My garment. Let us learn to soar!"

THE FIERY SHIELD

THE Mother of the World has proclaimed: "Winds, gather ye! Snows, gather ye! Birds, hold ye back! Beasts, stand ye back!

"No human foot shall set its traces on My Summit! The audacity of the dark ones shall not surmount!

"The light of the moon shall not endure! But the sun-ray shall touch the peak.

"Sun, guard My Summit! For where shall I keep My Vigil?

"Never shall beast ascend. Nor shall human power endure."

Herself, the Mother of all Being, shall keep Her Vigil, with a fiery shield.

What glows upon the Summit? Why have the whirl-winds assembled a resplendent crown?

She, the Great Mother, alone ascended the Summit.

And none may follow Her.

THE FIERY VEIL

UPON the highest summit stands effulgent the Mother of the World.

She came forth to smite the darkness.

Why are the enemies fallen? And whither do they turn their eyes in desperation?

She has cloaked Herself in a fiery mantle and encircled Herself in a fiery wall.

She is our Citadel and our Striving.

APOLLONIUS OF TYANA

THE VISIT OF APOLLONIUS TO THE NORTH OF INDIA

THE story preserved of the life of Apollonius contains the tale of his visit to the North of India. A precisely detailed description is given of the cities, the sites and the people; but the significance of his visit is completely overlooked. Truly, Apollonius of Tyana was known as a lover of distant travel. But this little explains his journeys.

While still a young man he heard of the existence and the Dwelling of the Brotherhood, from one who knew and collected strange tales. He paid little regard to it. But later when he knew more and had discerned more, he recalled it and in the depths of his spirit decided to visit the North of India.

He had a friend, a great scientist, who had received many degrees of initiation. And to him, Apollonius turned for advice. The old man became pensive and promised to obtain information.

And thus, after one year, the reply came. The old man addressed Apollonius, "My friend, happiness is truly with you. They write to me that you may prepare for your journey. In Kashmir you shall meet my friend. I deem he can give you necessary directions. Thus, prepare for your journey."

The journey of Apollonius was long. He encountered numerous people upon his way. One of those whom he met, as though surmising Apollonius's intention, said, "I can be useful to you. He to Whom you journey is known to Me. I beg you to use my house when you shall reach ancient Gandhara." And the stranger gave Apollonius a casket. Apollonius never learned the name of the stranger.

Reaching Taksila, Apollonius found the dwelling of the stranger, and approaching its doors knocked with the hammer. The door opened and a young Hindu invited Apollonius to enter. Only then did Apollonius recall that the name of the host was unknown to him. The door-keeper evidently awaited. In order to explain his arrival, Apollonius showed him the casket. The door-keeper made a gesture and let Apollonius into a room where stood a table and two arm-chairs.

Shortly the door opened and into the room entered a tall man, dressed in a kaftan with the insignia of a cavalry commander.

Calling himself brother to the host, and as if knowing the purpose of Apollonius's visit, he said, "My people shall accompany you tomorrow."

In the morning, in the courtyard, Apollonius saw several warriors and horses. They set out on their journey, hurrying towards the northern mountains.

There the warriors left Apollonius.

THE PASSING OF APOLLONIUS

IN the biography of Apollonius the tale of his passing is mutilated. But there remains the evidence of his pupil, Callicratus, concerning the last journey of the Teacher.

Apollonius began to hear voices bidding him return to those very shores where he had once been, to the great enrichment of his spirit. Taking with him his pupil Callicratus, the Teacher, without revealing the goal of his journey, set sail at once.

As they approached the Cave where the Great Teacher bestowed initiation upon the Arhats, a tall old man came forth to meet them. Long he conversed with Apollonius. Callicratus heard only the final word of the old man, "If thou hast decided to accept the chalice of Apostolate of the Teaching, do not delay."

When the old man disappeared into the recesses of the cave, Apollonius bid Callicratus hurriedly gather much of the fragrant wood and heap it up as a couch in the cave. He also indicated to Callicratus that when he would hear a voice issuing from the vault of the cave, to ignite the wood, without glancing back; then to hasten to the shores of Greece, forgetting what had occurred. Thereupon the Teacher sank into seeming sleep.

Callicratus sat motionless tending the fire, until late into the night, when high beneath the vault of the cave the greatly reverberant voice of the Teacher rang out: "And so I have not died, but I go to accept the chalice of Apostolate."

Thereupon Callicratus fulfilled all as he was bidden; and he bade them lay this testimony with him into the grave.

FROM THE LIFE OF
ST. SERGIUS OF RADONEGA

THE PROCLAMATION OF
THE MOTHER CELESTIAL

THE time has come to set forth the most Meaningful—the vision of glory of the Mother Celestial. Can it be that the great predestined vision was a silent one? Can it not be that the trembling of the spirit and the hoary head resulted from this great proclamation?

The Mother Celestial said, "My Time will come, when My Heavenly Star will speed earthward. Then wilt thou come to fulfil the ordinance of the dates.

"And the despised ones will be the saviors. And the vanquished one will lead the victors. And the three roots cleft by a curse will be knitted with love. And they will be led by a Messenger not of their strain. Until then will the Tartar and Jew be cursed, and they will curse the Russian soil.

"And when thy bones shall be scattered, the date of the three curses will be fulfilled. And invisibly visible, thou wilt be enthroned, adorned in thy Crown and a Signet-ring.

"And there where thou wilt set Thy Seal, there will My Hand be. And Those of the Lords."

SAYINGS OF SERGIUS

"IF one hears the voice of his spirit, he shall be borne above the precipice." Thus spoke Sergius.

"And he who departs into the forest cannot hear the speech of humans. And he who falls asleep will not hear the birds, heralds of the sun. And he who is silent before a manifested miracle shall pay penalty with his sight. And he who forbears to aid his brother shall not draw the thorn from his foot." Thus spoke Sergius.

To Sergius came Saint Alexis, questioning, "What is there to do?"

Sergius answered, "Help the Russian Soil!"

When the peasants asked Sergius, "What shall we do?" He answered, "Help the Russian Soil!"

When Minin addressed Sergius, came the answer: "Help the Russian Soil!"

THE TRAVAIL OF SERGIUS

GRAY is his beard. The Flaming Spirit attends Him in service. And the mighty Prince has already bowed before Him.

But should the bread-cart delay, the beloved brethren cannot sustain their faith for a single hour. Should his purse be momentarily depleted, then the worthy and chosen brethren are ready to barter the wondrous Bliss for a stranger's penny. They even add, "Your guardian saints have become poverty-stricken!"

And by day and by night, they await—not enlightenment, but the well-being of body.

Of Sergius it was said that during the dark night often he made his rounds through the cells and finding all deep in sleep he went further, nor roused them.

It may be that he hoped to find one among them vigilant!

FORESIGHT OF SERGIUS

SERGIUS sometimes also spoke of the White Mountain but never indicated its location.

And when somebody unexpectedly knocked, the brothers said, "Is it not the Abbott?"

Said Sergius, "Upon the White Mountain live diverse beings. When they have need they are two-headed and five-legged, not like ourselves. Their sleighs go without horses and in the need of haste they can fly."

AKBAR THE GREAT

THE SILVERY MESSENGER

BENEATH a tree Akbar beheld a vision. To him suddenly appeared a Silvery Messenger, who said, "For the first time and the last time thou here beholdest Me, as if I never appeared. Thou shalt build a Kingdom and in it a future Temple. And as a Ruler thou shalt traverse the field of life, bearing within thy spirit the future Temple.

"Verily, long hast thou traveled the path of God. It is need to end the earthly way. Thou shalt not hear My Voice. Nor shalt thou see My Light. And thou shalt guard thy readiness to walk the way of God.

"But when approaches the hour to unbar the next Gates, thy wife, ordained to thee by God, shall hear My Knock and shall say, 'He is at the Gates.' But thou shalt see Me only on the crossing of the border. And when thy wife shall enter the final way she shall behold thee in My Image.

"And thou, be a king on earth, and thereafter the landlord. And when thou endest thy earthly way encircle the fields of thy garden. Each departing one shall leave no crumbs upon the festal board. Traverse each overgrown path and remember: the nearer, the further. First in storm, then in gale, then in silence!"

Then the Messenger became illumined with a silvery glow and the leaves upon the trees became translucent as rainbows. And thereafter the air trembled. Then all became as before.

Akbar saw nothing ever again. When the hour of liberation arrived, he and his wife rejoiced that another date was approaching, the ordained date. For there exists no grave.

THE HELP OF HEAVEN

THE Ruler was convinced that at each difficult hour the help of heaven would come to him. Time came to declare war against the Princes of Golconda and the Ruler was perplexed over his decision. As the eye of the Ruler wandered over the floor he saw an ant bearing a great load. And the ant endured it long.

Finally Akbar exclaimed, "Why should one beset oneself with the burden of Golconda!" And he gave his command to cease preparations for the march.

Another time the Ruler attended a Court and wished to take part in pronouncing verdict. But his attention was drawn to the trembling of a butterfly, which beat its wings against the window. And he forgot the word that he had crystallized and thought, "Let the judges fulfil their duty," remarking aloud, "Today I am only a guest here."

And the verdict was justly merciful.

Enemies made attempts against the life of Akbar. An assassin stood ready behind a tree in the garden where the Ruler was walking alone. A black serpent crawled across the path and the Ruler turned back to summon his servants. Seeking for the serpent they discovered the assassin behind the tree.

Then the Ruler said, "The help of heaven crawls over the earth. Let only the eye and ear be open."

THE COMMANDERS

OF the two commanders of Akbar: One commander received most explicit indications; the other only the most fragmentary ones. Finally the latter addressed Akbar, saying, "Why have I not deserved explicit commands when I gathered so many victories?"

Akbar replied, "Your understanding restrained the flow of words. Let each moment saved by you be commemorated with the most precious pearl."

Therefore, surpassing is the joy of those who can understand, saving the draught of the source.

Let us add about the third commander. He asked, "Why are tardiness and prematurity equally condemned?"

Akbar replied, "My friend, there are no equal values. Hence, if prematurity comprises resourcefulness, its merit is greater because tardiness is linked only with death. Prematurity is to be adjudged; but tardiness is already condemned."

Surrounded and threatened, Akbar addressed his commanders: "The less agitated is the substance, the more clear is the reflection of the summits."

After inspecting his army, Akbar said, "A fourth part is already achieved. I have seen satisfied people. The rest we shall see after a day of heat, after a day of rain, after a sleepless night."

ENEMIES

AKBAR, called Great, regarded his enemies with care. His beloved councilor kept a list of enemies. Akbar often inquired, has not some worthy name found its way to the list?

"When I see a worthy name I shall send my greeting to a friend in disguise."

And Akbar further said, "I rejoice that I could apply the sacred Teaching in life, that I could give to people of plenty, and that I was shaded by great enemies."

Thus spoke Akbar, knowing the value of enemies.

During the assaults of his enemies Akbar was asked why there were so many attacks.

Akbar replied, "Allow to the enemies moments of being occupied with something."

INVISIBLY VISIBLE

THE Court Historian of Akbar once said to the Ruler, "Among potentates I observed an insoluble problem. Certain rulers held themselves unapproachable, aloof from the people. These were deposed because of their futility. Others entered into the daily lives. People became used to them and deposed them for being commonplace."

Akbar smiled. "That means that a Ruler must remain unseen, but entering and directing all actions."

Thus ordained the wise Ruler, foretelling thereby the future.

Invisibly visible!

LEGENDS AND LORE

A TALE OF COSMOGONY

THE Hindu tale of cosmogony recounts as follows:

There once lived a deadly monster that devoured people. Once the monster pursued his marked victim. The man, seeking to save himself, dove into a lake. The monster followed. Still seeking safety, the swimmer leaped on the hack of the monster and tightly seized the upright comb.

The monster could not turn over because his belly was unguarded. It started to rush about in a raging flight, anticipating that the man would become exhausted.

But the man bethought himself that by his own desperate plight he was saving humanity. And under this universal vision his strength became intense, unfatigued.

Meanwhile the monster increased his speed until sparks formed a fiery wake. And amid the flame, the monster started to rise above the earth. The universal thought of the man had raised up even the enemy.

When men see a comet they are grateful to the valiant one, eternally striving. The thoughts of people hasten on, giving new force to the rider of the monster.

White, yellow, red, and black peoples turn their thoughts to him who long since became aflame.

THE MESSENGER OF LIGHT

A N ancient legend recounts:
From a far-off world came a Messenger to bestow upon men Equality, Brotherhood, and Joy. Long since had men forgotten their songs. They remained in a stupor of hate.

The Messenger banished darkness and narrowness of the human crowd. He effaced contagion and raised up joyous labor. Hatred was bridled and the sword of the Messenger remained upon the wall. But all were silent and could not sing.

Then the Messenger gathered the little children and took them into the forest, saying, "These are your flowers, your streams, your trees. No one has followed us. I shall rest—and be you filled with joy." Thereupon timidly they ventured into the forest.

At last the smallest of them remained on the green, lost in rapture at beholding the sun's rays. Then the yellow oriole started its call. The little one followed it, whispering; then soon, joyously he exclaimed, "The sun is ours!"

One by one, the children returned to the green and a new hymn to light rang out.

The Messenger said, "Man has again begun to sing. Come is the date!"

SEVEN SERVANTS

HERE, we shall send seven servants to market to bring some grapes.

What do I see? The first lost the money. The second exchanged it for intoxicating wine. The third hid it. The fourth did not notice that the grapes were green. The fifth, testing their ripeness, crushed the entire branch. The sixth chose wisely but brushed them and scattered them through carelessness. The seventh brought a ripe branch and even found leaves to adorn it.

Thus did seven pass along one road and at the same time.

THE CITADEL OF LOYALTY

THE Ruler asked a sage, "How shall one distinguish the nest of treason from the citadel of loyalty?"

The sage pointed to a group of richly dressed riders and said: "A nest of treason."

Then he indicated a solitary traveler and said, "A citadel of loyalty. Because naught can betray solitude."

And henceforth the Ruler surrounded himself with loyalty.

REVERENCE TO THE TEACHER

I RECALL a small Hindu who found his Teacher. We asked him, "Is it possible that the sun would shine to you if you would see it without the Teacher?"

The boy smiled: "The sun would remain as the sun but in the presence of the Teacher twelve suns would shine to me!"

The sun of wisdom of India shall shine because upon the shores of a river there sits a boy who knows the Teacher.

MILAREPA

THE Teacher Milarepa often discoursed with animals. Near his retreat were hiving bees; ants erected their cities; parrots flew about; and a monkey was accustomed to sit like the Teacher.

The Teacher said to the ants: "Tillers and builders, none knows of you, yet you raise up lofty communities."

He said to the bees: "Gather the honey of knowledge and of the best images. None shall interrupt your sweet toil."

To the parrot he said: "By your shrieks I perceive that you are preparing yourself to be a judge and preacher."

Shaking his finger at the mischievous monkey, he said: "You demolished the constructions of the ant; you stole honey that is not yours. Perhaps you have decided to become a ruler!"

THE HERMIT

THREE mice approached a hermit, attracted by his motionlessness. He addressed each one: "Thou livest in the flour. Although there are enough provisions for all thy kind, thou didst not improve.

"Thou hast chosen thy habitation in books and hast gnawed great numbers of them, but thou didst not become wiser.

"Thou livest amidst sacred objects, but didst not become exalted.

"Verily, mice, you can become humans. Like people you defile the given treasures."

Three lions came to the hermit. He addressed each one: "Thou hast but now killed a traveler who hastened to his family.

"Thou hast robbed a blind woman of her single sheep.

"Thou hast done away with the horse of an important messenger.

"Lions, you can become humans. Don your terrifying manes and begin war. Do not wonder if people will appear more cruel than you."

Three doves came flying to the hermit. He addressed each one: "Thou hast pecked grain not thine own and hast considered it thine.

"Thou hast pecked a healing plant and art revered as a sacred bird.

"Thou hast built thy nest in a temple not thine own and in the name of superstition, thou hast forced another to feed thee.

"Verily, doves, it is time for you to become humans. Superstition and bigotry will plentifully feed you."

BATUR-BAKSHA

Batur-Baksha came to tell to the people the word of Truth.

Said Batur to his comrades, "I shall tell the entire word of Truth." His comrades became terrified. "Let us better say half of the Truth. Otherwise the firm earth will not endure."

But Batur may not tarry. He goes forth to tell the entire word of Truth. The serpent has become a black arrow. The serpent strikes the center of Batur's bosom. The word of truth is untold.

Batur shall be buried, to the sorrow of all people. But Batur himself does not die of the serpent. He leaves only his armor in the coffin. And he secretly departs into the fields. "I shall go forth to search new comrades who will not fear the entire word of Truth."

Batur passes over mountains and through deserts. As a sun, burns the entire word of Truth. Batur becomes blanched from the searing heat of Truth.

Himself, the Ruler of Shambhala, hails Batur: "Ho, Batur. I shall bestow upon thee one of My own names. I will give thee new comrades. They shall not be bowed down from the entire word of Truth.

"Ascend thou the Mountain Adighan. Turn to the South. When thou shalst see the mighty dust; when thou shalst perceive spears; when thou shalst number the steeds; then I Myself am coming. Yamuchi himself follows me.

"Hasten! Wherefore to turn back? Look to the South! Come is the word of Truth!"

Thus do they sing in the depths of Asia.

But Batur Baksha has not died. He searches for new comrades who do not fear the entire word of Truth.

THE WHITE MOUNTAIN

THE White Mountain it was which knew whence came the white water.

The Mountain shall send its stones to Katun. The stones are washing away the White shores. The stones set brother against brother. Red as of blood is Katun. War continues.

White Mountain, did you send red stones? Where are your White Waters?

I shall take a cedar staff. I shall don a white garment; and I shall ascend the White Mountain. I shall ask Her—Whence came the White Water?

Out of the mountain, from the very peak itself, emerged manifold peaks. Beyond them glimmers the White Mountain.

Is it the Stone that glows? Disclosed is the Mystery.

Let us hence, brothers, to that resplendent glow!

Seen is the never-seen; audible is the never-audible.

Upon a White Mountain stands the city. Heard is the peal of bells. The cock crows upon the appointed day.

Let us retire into the City and harken to the Great Book.

ARROWS OF THOUGHTS

L ET us regard the stars. We were told that the vessel of wisdom poured from out of Tushita and the drops of the miraculous draught became aglow in space.

But the Teacher said, "Thus glow the tips of the arrows of thought because thought pierces the radiant substance and creates worlds."

Creative thought! Do not cease to adorn space with the flowers of light.

THE THOUGHT OF THE WORLD

SAID Solomon: "I shall set thee at the crossroad and shall make thee silent and unmovable.

"Before thee shall pass the signs of events.

"Thus shalst thou restrain thy human curiosity.

"Thus shalst thou peer into the predestined tide of the current.

Because beyond the human is borne the thought of the world."

Thus mark the flow of events, as though from the top of a tower thou numbereth thy flocks of sheep.

THE SOURCE OF PATIENCE

"LORD of the Seven Gates, lead us sunwards, who have passed through midnight.

"Thine are our arrows, O Lord.

"Without Thy Command we shall not enter the city of rest.

"Neither an hour nor a day nor a year will arrest our way.

"Because Thou, the most speedy, holdest the reins of our horses.

"Because Thou, also, hast passed this way and gave Thy patience as guarantee.

"Say, Keeper, whence flows the source of Patience?"

"Out of the ore of trust."

Who knows when the messenger changes his steed?

THE KEEPER OF THE SEVEN GATES

GRIEVED the Keeper of the Seven Gates: "I have visited people with an endless stream of miracles. But they do not perceive them.

"I provide new stars. But their light does not alter human thought.

"I plunge whole countries into the depths of the seas. But human consciousness is stilled.

"I erect mountains and the Teachings of Truth. But people do not even turn their heads at the call.

"I send wars and pestilence. But even terror does not impel people to think.

"I offer the joy of knowledge. But people make a gruel out of the sacred feast.

"I have no further signs to hold humanity from destruction."

To the Keeper came the Most Exalted: "When the builder lays the foundations of the building, does he proclaim it to all who labor on the structure? The least of these knows the determined measures.

"Only to few is disclosed the purpose of the building. Those who dig the stones of past foundations will not comprehend a single new foundation.

"But the builder should not grieve if there be no realization among his workers of the real import of the design. He can only distribute the work in proportion."

Thus in the consciousness of people we shall know that those who cannot contain nor harken shall fulfil only the lowest labor.

Let him who understood be firm as a hundred thousand sages. And the signs, as inscriptions, shall unfold before him.

THE FLAMING ONE

THE Flaming One addressed the Prince of Darkness: "Thou hast poisoned the air. Thou hast polluted the waters. Thou hast depleted the earth. But fire thou hast not touched. Nor hast the fire touched thee. And fire shall burn thee as light smiteth darkness. The Great Flame is untiring. And thou shalt not dare to emerge from thy dwelling.

"From space shall I evoke new fires which shall wither thy works. As sterile fissures. As desiccated bones. Thus shalt thou be confounded, cast hence, and retreat.

"The wall of flame shall approach thee; nor shalt thou find therein thy marks. By the far-off worlds shall I guard the flame. Thou canst not poison, nor pollute, nor deplete it.

"I shall summon the fiery host, born amidst fire. They shall not succumb. And the waters evoked by thee shall not quench their burning.

"Prince of the Darkness, beware of the fire!"

THE GIFT OF DARKNESS

THE Spirit of Darkness pondered how still more firmly to lash humanity to earth. "Let them preserve their customs and habits. Nothing so binds humanity to earth as forms of habit.

"But this means is fit only for the masses. Far more dangerous is solitude. Then the consciousness is illumined and new forms are created.

"One must limit the hours of solitude. People must not remain alone. I shall provide them with a reflection and let them become used to their image."

The servants of darkness brought to the people—a mirror!

THE REWARD

A MAN gave much gold for good works. But he awaited reward. Once his Teacher sent him a stone with the message: "Accept the reward, the Treasure of the far-off star."

The man became indignant: "Instead of my gold a stone is given me. What is a far-off star to me?" And in dejection he cast the stone into a mountain stream.

But the Teacher came and said, "How did you find the treasure? In the stone was contained the most precious diamond, sparkling beyond all earthly gems."

In despair the man rushed to the stream. And following the current he descended lower and lower.

But the ripples of the waves forever hid the treasure.

TWO PITRIS

TWO of humanity's elders quarreled about man. The one of Light declared that man would give up everything.

But the Dark One protested that man would conceal something for himself.

They began to test man. They bereft him of all things until, like a savage, he wandered garbed in a torn rag.

"Behold, he renounced all and lives!" the Light One pointed out.

"Wait awhile," derided the Dark One, and he threw upon the road a weeping child.

The man covered the child with his last rag and shed a tear.

"Behold, he renounced everything," declared the Light One.

But the Dark One answered, "Yes, he renounced his rag. But his heart is guarded."

Thus, the Dark One outwitted the Light One.

PRINCE OF DARKNESS

LUCIFER

WHEREIN lay the revolt of Lucifer? He wished to remain within the boundaries of the planet. And the legend of the Prince of the World is fairly true.

He began to surround himself with spirits content with the earthly aura. In order to hold his followers he began to unfold before them the possibilities of earth, imitating—at times with skill—the counterposition of the opposing side.

One may speak of the miracles of the Antichrist. "Wherefore is needed the realization of the future, when I can show you the forces of earth!"

But among his followers, none will say on departing from earth: "I ascend, Lord!" Instead they tremble, rending themselves from the earthly effulgence.

Truly beautiful was Lucifer, and he imparted to people in his way the understanding of the earthly radiance. But without him there would not be a definite boundary between the earth and the nearest spheres. Without him the difference between life on earth and on other spheres would be gradually effaced, permitting to incarnate spirits the movability of matter.

But the ancient Prince of the World, in opposition, chains matter to the crust occupied by him. As the planetary spirit, he knew the depths of the earth. But his error lies in the unwillingness of cooperation with other planets. Precisely this is what brought Christ to the World.

While Lucifer glorifies the life of earth, Christ points to the beauty of the entire Creation of the worlds.

We say, "Let the light of Lucifer glow, but the greatness of other fires cannot be hidden behind it." We do not fear to pronounce his name. We are aware of his existence.

We say, "Your way cannot fulfil the destiny of earth because only through communion with other worlds will the life of your stronghold be regenerated. Your rocks will wear away and whereon then will you set your throne? And the eternal life and the eternal flux give us an eternal home. Christ in no way differed from your servants but He showed the privilege of motion beyond the boundaries of earth." Christ said, "I may spend the night upon the beautiful earth in order to continue the journey; but thou, host of the earth, bid thy servants back, lest they prevent me from going my way at dawn."

And thus, one became ensnared by matter, the other passed on to the worlds of possibilities of Light.

Lucifer, come is the time to re-kindle your lamp!

Lucifer, who might have become the expounder of Unity, preferred to sever himself from his neighbors. The battle of desperation transformed the Bearer of Light; and the ruby aura became infused with the blood-red glow. His followers truly began to apply depraved means.

Miserable Carrier of Light! In the death of Christ you admitted an irrevocable error. The cedar of Lebanon which bore the body of Christ shall but shorten the way to the Highest World. Hence you shall have to depart to Saturn; for this, have you long been called *Satan*. But there also shall the gardener of matter find fields to labor as on earth. And accept Our last counsel. Look over the rows of your servants!

Upon the ladder of life you sought to outdistance the Teacher. Be warned: Here stands She, witness of your destiny. The Star of the Mother of the World rose as a signal against your madness, when you determined to demean Her, the Bearer of Spirit.

You will behold woman return to her destined place.

GOLD AND DARKNESS

GOLD

THE gas destructive to the planet is disclosed.

It is contained in pure gold. One must keep it back. Naturally, stones and metals mostly bind men with the depths of the planet and become nests of contagion.

The widespread worship of gold has compelled us to pay attention to it. By the means of complicated research, attempts were made to apply the action of gold to various manifestations of Cosmic forces.

There is no doubt that this metal was especially saturated with powerful light emissions. And the gold veins transmit the astral light to the bottoms of earth. Hence, if the astral world is well-ordered, the role of gold may even be beneficent.

But precisely this conductor can become a fuse to the explosion.

One may imagine how easily this metal can transmit the brown gas which is made dense by the horror of the astral world. And the spirit will make its appearance as an exploder and an impetus for volcanos.

DARKNESS

ABSOLUTE darkness is the constant antipode of light. It is the enemy of all which exists. It is the negation of life. It is the strangler and poisoner.

Then, what is it? It is the ejection of the imperfect spirit. There are not words fit to describe this pressure and this suffocation. Not many could look upon this enemy of the planet without becoming ill.

It is precisely this darkness that begins to leave its previous depositories. Upon its way it corrodes all elements and the gas forces the elements of destruction into these fissures.

LEGEND OF THE STONE

LEGEND OF THE STONE

THROUGH the desert I come—I bring the Chalice covered with the Shield.

Within it is a treasure—the Gift of Orion.

O Thou Flame-bearer, remember Lob-Nor and spread Thy tents. Kuku-Nor—the steed hastens.

And in the temple of Judaea, the "Flame-bearer" tarried not. And barely did Passedvan save It; with him It left the ruins of China behind.

Reach not for the Stone, Lun; It will come of Itself if thou knowest to await It.

But by treason the servants of the temple usurped the Stone from the Ruler of India to glorify a foreign land.

Let the mountain of pride conceal for a while the Stone. Let the city of the Stone be glorified. But the path of the treasure is ordained.

It is time for the Stone to return homewards.

When above the chalice the flame shall coil in a ring then My time approaches.

On the Island of Lanka lieth the Stone hidden through the treachery of Ravanna. It will depart beyond the sea.

In its wake, like the tail of a comet, happiness is still ablaze; but not for long.

Let the hundred steps of China greet the "Flame-bearer." But Passedvan bears away the Stone. And the sands transmit the Fire to the dauntless horseman, Timur. The great one approached the wall of Amber and covered the field with his banners.

"Let the Stone rest in the Temple until my return."

But life brought the miracle to the grandson. The way of the Stone turned westward.

Under the ground are assembled the religious fathers to analyze the nature of the Stone. Why, when the Stone becomes dark, do the clouds gather? When the Stone feels heavy, blood is shed. When a star shines over the Stone, comes success. When the Stone creaks, the enemy approaches. When comes a dream of fire over the Stone, the world is convulsed. When the Stone is tranquil, walk courageously. But do not pour wine over the Stone! Burn over it only cedar-balsam. Carry the Stone in an ivory casket.

As one must be accustomed to heat and to cold, so must one become accustomed to the radiance of the Stone. Each of the bearers of the Stone must abide with it tranquilly awhile. The intoxication from Its rays is unseen but Its inner heat is mightier than radium. Unseen flows the Myrrh but the Stone rests visible upon the web of Its native land.

Amidst the breath of the steppe and the crystal resonance of the mountains the spirit of the Stone marks the way of the banner. The miracle of Orion's rays is guiding the people. To the tall Yutzakis and Karakorum-Nor the Teacher will lead the steeds. At Uyub-Nor the manifestation is awaited.

Priestly knowledge of all time prepared men for the worthy reception of the Treasure. Long since have wisdom's laws revealed the day when a dual eclipse and the submersion of the sanctities would mark the new advent of the Stone. Let us in prayer await our destiny!

Oh, Stone, start hence over the sea. Let the bird bring to the ear the tiding: The Stone cometh.

In the darkness of the night darkly attired, the messenger noiselessly approaches to perceive how they await. Around the bend of the corner lies in wait the tamed beast, sniffing, groping with his paw; he is sent by the enemy. Who stirs behind the casement? What flies are swarming the place? Whence blows this whirlwind? But I walk firmly and securely: I am holding the Stone. I am learning the prayer: "Forsake me not, my Lord. I have gathered all strength. Forsake me not for I come unto Thee!"

On Mount Ararat lies the fiery Stone. A knight of Novgorod killed himself over the Stone because of unbelief. The great freedom of Novgorod proved the possession of the treasure but heresy diverted the fulfilment of the miracle.

The best relic of the power of the Stone is symbolized by the serpent's Stone—symbol of a wise possession.

The follower of night sought to regain possession of the Stone. But the Treasure was ever the token of Light. Not for long did sly rulers possess the Stone, being unaware that striving for right alone can rule the fire of the Stone.

Uroil Zena, spirit of the air, bore to King Solomon the Stone. Proclaimed the Spirit into the receptive ear: "By the will of the Lord of Powers I entrust unto thee the treasure of the Lord of Powers. I entrust unto thee the treasure of the world."

"So be it," said the King and carried the Stone into the Temple. But the thought possessed him to carry part of the treasure on his person. Then the King summoned Ephraim, the goldsmith of the tribe of Judah; he bade him sever a part of the Stone and take pure silver and weld a ring and engrave upon the Stone the chalice of wisdom illumined with a flame. The King thought never to part with the Treasure. But the spirit said, "Not wisely didst thou violate the supreme A-Substance. It shall be sorely difficult for the sons of men to possess the Stone. And only those who are with thee can direct the Stone to righteousness. By a constellation shall I designate the way of the Stone."

Departed is the envoy to Khan Tamerlane. Uneasily lies the Stone at Otakuye. A guard of three banners must be dispatched. Upon camels men are journeying. A pillar of sand obscures the sun. The elements conceal the travelers. Endlessly they wander. And the Kayuks turn their steeds homewards. At night, who will safeguard the Stone? The desert hid the strangers and with them the Stone went to the south. Reflect, Khan, how to overtake the Stone righteously. Came sorrow and disease; the steed even loses its footing. To the worthy horsemen came the manifested Spirit: "Search not. Time alone will reveal the way." Each Ulus sings its own song about the Stone.

Father Sulpicius beheld a vision: A white pillar of clouds appeared to him. From it issued a Voice: "Keep the Stone in the shrine brought from Rothenburg. Upon it are four squares and in each the sign 'M'. The manifestation will be revealed when I shall pronounce: "The march of the four eastward!" Naught shall lessen the commandment. Yield to the destined hour. I shall assemble the warriors of My star. Whosoever are ordained to recognize the appointed time, they shall gather. This I attest by this hour, that the Stone is shaped like a human heart and within it is enshrined a resplendent crystal." At these words the pillar dispersed into blue sparks, casting Father Sulpicius into incomparable tremor. Herein is the greater wonder, that the Stone which came from the East has the shape of a flat fruit or heart, oblong in form. Upon the shrine were found the foretold letters. Unknown is their meaning.

The Ruler Kurnovoo, laden with gold, received from Tazlavoo the dark Stone containing the crystal of life. And over the gold the Ruler wore the Stone.

Out of the book of Tristan, called Lun: "When the Son of the Sun descended upon earth to teach mankind, there fell from heaven a Shield which bore the power of the world. In the center of the Shield between the three distinct marks were signs of silver predicting events under the rays of the sun. The sudden darkening of the sun threw into despair the Son of the Sun and he dropped and shattered the Shield. For ominous was the constellation. But the power remained in the central fragment—there the ray of the Sun touched. It is said that King Solomon severed the central portion of the Stone for his ring. The legend of our priests also tells of the shattered shield of the sun. It is a most grievous error to deny the Stone. Verily, I myself have seen this fragment of the world—I recall its shape—the length of my little finger—of grayish luster like a dried fruit. Even the signs I remember but did not understand them. Truly I myself have seen the Stone and I shall find It. It is said that the Stone comes of Itself; It cannot be taken. If so, I shall await It. For Its sake I shall take myself to the desert, until the end of my days."

Remember, Lun, you decided to await It!

When the Stone was lost from the Ruler of India, his wife said, "We shall find It again. The courageous one demandeth a bow, himself to mark down the bird!"

When the Emperor of China possessed the treasure of the sun, he erected for It a turquoise temple of the color of the azure sky. When the little princes with the bride peered behind the door for a long time, the Emperor said, "The fox is leading you. You feel the joy of the world."

Remember the iron crown of the Longbards; that, too, is a trace of the Stone. Not long did the Stone rest near the mountain of pride. Many are the envoys from the East. The camels bring the Stone to Tibet. Across the desert they carry It and with It a new power.

And Its last flight to the West lighted up an unheard-of kingdom of an unsuccessful union of western nations. In each ray of the East they already seek the Stone. The time will come; the dates will be fulfilled. Designated is the ordained way when of Itself the Stone will come from the West. We affirm to await and understand the way of the Stone. We affirm to understand the predestined carriers of the Stone who go homewards. The ship is ready.

The New Country shall go forth to meet the seven stars under the sign of three stars which sent the Stone to the world. Prepared is the treasure and the enemy shall not take the Shield covered with gold.

Await the Stone!

PROPHECIES OF SHAMBHALA
AND MAITREYA

PROPHECIES OF SHAMBHALA
AND MAITREYA

THE Treasure is returning from the West. On the mountains the fires of jubilation are kindled. Behold the road! There walk those who carry the Stone. Upon the Shrine are the signs of Maitreya.

Out of the Sacred Kingdom is given the date when the carpet of expectation may be spread. By the sign of the seven stars shall the Gates be opened.

"By fire shall I manifest My messengers. Gather the prophecies of your happiness."

Thus are fulfilled the prophecies of the ancestors and the writings of the wise ones.

Gather thy understanding to hail the Predestined, when in the Fifth Year the heralds of the warriors of Northern Shambhala shall appear. Gather understanding to meet them. And receive the New Glory!

I shall manifest My Sign of Lightning!

Kesar-khan indicates, "I have many treasures but only upon the appointed day may I bestow them upon My People. When the legions of Northern Shambhala shall bring the Spear of Salvation then shall I uncover the depths of the mountains and you shall divide My treasures equally among the warriors and yourselves and live in justice. The time shall soon come for that command of Mine: to cross all deserts.

"When My gold was scattered by the winds I ordained the day when the people of Northern Shambhala would come to gather My possessions.

"Then shall My people prepare their bags for the treasures. And to each shall I give a just share."

"One may find sands of gold. One may find precious gems. But the true wealth shall come only with the people of Northern Shambhala when the time is come to send them forth.

"Thus is ordained."

The approaching Maitreya is symbolized with His feet set upon earth—the symbol of haste.

It is predicted that the manifestation of Maitreya will come after the wars. But the final war will be for the True Teaching.

But each one rising up against Shambhala shall be stricken in all his works. And the waves shall wash away his dwelling. And even a dog will not answer to his call. Not clouds but lightning shall he see on the final night. And the red messenger shall rise up on pillars of Light.

The teaching indicates that each warrior of Shambhala shall be named the invincible.

The Lord Himself hastens and His banner is already above the mountains!

The Blessed Buddha bestowed upon you the cherished Maitreya to approach the New Era. Thy Pastures shall reach the Promised Land.

When thou tendest thy flocks, dost thou not hear the voices of the stones? These are the toilers of Maitreya who make ready the treasures for thee.

When the wind murmureth through the reeds, dost thou understand that this is the arrows of Maitreya flying in protection?

When lightning illumineth thy camps, knowest thou that this is the light of thy desired Maitreya?

To whom shall the watch upon the first night be entrusted?—To thee!

To whom shall My envoys be despatched?—To thee! Who shall meet them?—Thou!

From the West, from the mountains, shall come My People. Who shall receive and safeguard them?—Thou!

Beseech the Tara to rest with thee. Determine to cleanse thy hearts until My Coming.

Each one hearing My desire shall cover his fur-cap with a red cover and shall entwine the head-strap of his horse with a red cord.

Look sharply upon the rings of the coming ones. There where is My chalice, there is salvation.

Upon the mountain, fires are kindled, coming is the New Year. Whoever shall out-slumber it shall not again awaken.

Northern Shamhhala is come!

We know not fear. We know not depression.

Dukhar, the many-eyed and many-armed, send us pure thoughts!

Ponder with deep thoughts. Ponder with thoughts of light.

One—two—three! I see three peoples.

One—two—three! I see three books. The first is of the Blessed One Himself. The second is given by Asvagosha. The third is given by Tzong kha pa.

One—two—three! I see three books of the coming of Maitreya. The first is written in the West. The second is written in the East. The third is written in the North.

One—two—three! I see three manifestations. The first is with the sword. The second is with the law. The third is with the light.

One—two—three! I see three horses. The first is black. The second is red. The third is white.

One—two—three! I see three ships. The first is on the waters. The second is under the waters. The third is above the earth.

One—two—three! I see three eagles. The first is perched upon the stone. The second is pecking his prey. The third is flying towards the sun.

One—two—three! I see the seekers of light. Red ray, blue ray, ray of silvery-white.

I affirm that the Teaching issued from Boddhigaya and shall return there.

When the procession carrying the Image of Shambhala shall pass through the lands of Buddha and return to the first source, then shall arrive the time of the pronunciation of the sacred word of *Shambhala*.

Then shall one receive merit from the pronouncement

of this Name. Then shall the thought of Shambhala provide sustenance.

Then shall the affirmation of Shambhala become the source of all works, and gratitude to Shambhala their end.

Great and small shall be filled with understanding of the Teaching.

Sacred Shambhala is pictured in impenetrable armor, amidst swords and spears.

Solemnly I affirm: Shambhala is invincible!

Fulfilled is the circle of the bearing of the Image! In the sites of Buddha; in the sites of Maitreya is brought the Image. Pronounced is "Kalagiya," as the banner of the Image unfurls.

What has been said is as true as that under the stone of Ghum lies the prophecy of Sacred Shambhala.

The Banner of Shambhala shall encircle the central lands of the Blessed One. Those who accept Him shall rejoice. And those who deny him shall tremble.

The Tashi Lama shall ask the Great Dalai Lama: "What is predestined for the last Dalai Lama?"

"The denier shall be given over to justice and shall be forgotten. And the warriors shall march under the banner of Maitreya. And the city of Lhassa shall be obscured and deserted.

"Those rising against Shambhala shall be cast down. To the obscured ones the Banner of Maitreya shall flow as blood over the lands of the new world. To those who have understood, as a red sun."

The Tashi Lama shall find the Great Dalai Lama and the Great Dalai Lama shall thus address him: "I will send thee the worthiest sign of my lightning. Go, overtake Tibet! The ring shall guard thee."

CPSIA information can be obtained
at www.ICGtesting.com
Printed in the USA
JSHW030927230223
38104JS00005B/86